EMMANUEL JOSEPH

Fashioning a Better World, The Ecology and Ethics of What We Wear

Copyright © 2025 by Emmanuel Joseph

All rights reserved. No part of this publication may be reproduced, stored or transmitted in any form or by any means, electronic, mechanical, photocopying, recording, scanning, or otherwise without written permission from the publisher. It is illegal to copy this book, post it to a website, or distribute it by any other means without permission.

First edition

This book was professionally typeset on Reedsy. Find out more at reedsy.com

Contents

1	Chapter 1: Introduction to Fashion's Impact	1
2	Chapter 2: The Birth of Fast Fashion	3
3	Chapter 3: The Environmental Toll of Textile Production	5
4	Chapter 4: The Human Cost of Fashion	7
5	Chapter 5: Sustainable Fashion Movements	8
6	Chapter 6: Innovations in Sustainable Materials	10
7	Chapter 7: The Role of Technology in Fashion	12
8	Chapter 8: The Power of Consumer Choice	14
9	Chapter 9: The Role of Fashion Brands	16
10	Chapter 10: The Importance of Ethical Sourcing	18
11	Chapter 11: The Future of Fashion	20
12	Chapter 12: Fashion Activism and Advocacy	22
13	Chapter 13: Redefining Luxury Fashion	24
14	Chapter 14: The Impact of Fashion on Culture	26
15	Chapter 15: Education and Empowerment in Fashion	27
16	Chapter 16: Fashion's Role in Climate Action	29
17	Chapter 17: Conclusion - Fashioning a Better World	31

1

Chapter 1: Introduction to Fashion's Impact

Fashion is an expression of culture, identity, and individualism, yet its influence extends far beyond aesthetics. As an industry, it is one of the world's largest, generating trillions of dollars annually. However, the glitz and glamor often obscure a darker reality. The environmental footprint of the fashion industry is massive, with textile production being one of the leading contributors to pollution. It consumes vast amounts of water and energy and generates significant waste and greenhouse gas emissions.

Beyond environmental concerns, the ethical implications of fashion are profound. The industry relies heavily on labor-intensive processes often carried out in developing countries where workers' rights are frequently violated. From sweatshops with deplorable conditions to unfair wages and child labor, the human cost of our clothing is staggering. The push for fast fashion exacerbates these issues, prioritizing speed and cost-efficiency over sustainability and ethical practices.

Consumers play a critical role in this ecosystem. Our choices drive demand, which in turn dictates production practices. By understanding the broader impact of our wardrobe decisions, we can become more mindful shoppers. This book seeks to explore the complex relationship between fashion, ecology, and ethics, offering insights and practical steps towards a more sustainable and just fashion industry.

As we embark on this journey, it is essential to recognize that fashion is not inherently harmful. It can be a force for good, fostering creativity, economic growth, and cultural exchange. The key lies in reimagining how we produce and consume clothing, ensuring that it respects both people and the planet.

2

Chapter 2: The Birth of Fast Fashion

The concept of fast fashion emerged in the late 20th century, revolutionizing how we purchase and wear clothing. The goal was to bring the latest trends from the runway to the retail floor in record time, making fashion accessible and affordable to the masses. Brands like Zara and H&M pioneered this approach, drastically shortening the design-to-shelf cycle.

This shift had profound implications for the industry. To keep up with the rapid turnaround, manufacturers outsourced production to countries with lower labor costs. This globalization of the supply chain led to a dramatic increase in clothing production. However, it also meant that environmental and labor standards were often compromised in the race to cut costs and maximize profits.

The rise of fast fashion also changed consumer behavior. Clothing became a disposable commodity, with low prices encouraging frequent purchases and discarding of garments. This throwaway culture contributes to the growing problem of textile waste, as millions of tons of clothing end up in landfills each year.

Despite its popularity, the fast fashion model is not sustainable in the long term. It places enormous strain on natural resources and exacerbates social inequalities. As awareness of these issues grows, consumers and brands alike are beginning to question the sustainability of fast fashion and explore alternatives that prioritize ethical and environmental considerations.

3

Chapter 3: The Environmental Toll of Textile Production

Textile production is one of the most resource-intensive processes in the fashion industry. It begins with the cultivation of raw materials, such as cotton, which requires vast amounts of water and pesticides. For instance, producing a single cotton T-shirt can consume up to 2,700 liters of water, equivalent to what one person drinks in two and a half years.

Synthetic fibers like polyester, derived from petroleum, present another set of environmental challenges. Their production is energy-intensive and contributes to the depletion of fossil fuels. Moreover, synthetic fabrics release microplastics during washing, which ultimately pollute our oceans and harm marine life.

The dyeing and finishing stages of textile production are also environmentally damaging. These processes involve toxic chemicals that often find their way into water systems, affecting both aquatic ecosystems and human health. The fashion industry is responsible for approximately 20% of global wastewater, highlighting the need for more sustainable practices.

Efforts to mitigate the environmental impact of textile production are gaining momentum. Innovations in sustainable fabrics, such as organic cotton, hemp, and recycled fibers, are becoming more prevalent. Additionally, advancements in dyeing technologies aim to reduce water and chemical usage.

By supporting these initiatives, consumers can help drive the industry towards more eco-friendly practices.

4

Chapter 4: The Human Cost of Fashion

Behind the glitz and glamour of the fashion industry lies a workforce often subjected to harsh and exploitative conditions. Garment workers, primarily in developing countries, are the backbone of the industry. Yet, they frequently endure long hours, low wages, and unsafe working environments.

The demand for cheap, fast fashion drives many of these issues. To meet tight deadlines and low-cost requirements, factories cut corners on safety and labor standards. Workers may face exposure to harmful chemicals, inadequate breaks, and physical strain. In some cases, child labor is still a grim reality.

High-profile tragedies, such as the Rana Plaza collapse in Bangladesh in 2013, have brought global attention to these injustices. The disaster, which killed over 1,100 workers, highlighted the urgent need for improved safety regulations and fair labor practices within the industry.

Consumer awareness and advocacy play a crucial role in driving change. By choosing brands that prioritize ethical practices and demanding transparency in the supply chain, shoppers can help ensure that the people who make our clothes are treated with dignity and respect. Supporting organizations that fight for workers' rights and calling for stronger regulations are also essential steps towards a fairer fashion industry.

5

Chapter 5: Sustainable Fashion Movements

In response to the growing concerns about the fashion industry's impact, various sustainable fashion movements have emerged. These initiatives aim to address environmental and ethical issues, promoting practices that respect both people and the planet.

The slow fashion movement advocates for a more thoughtful approach to clothing consumption. It encourages consumers to invest in high-quality, timeless pieces that are designed to last, rather than chasing fleeting trends. This shift can reduce the volume of clothing produced and discarded, easing the strain on natural resources.

The circular fashion movement focuses on creating a closed-loop system where garments are designed, produced, and recycled in a way that minimizes waste. This approach emphasizes the importance of materials that can be reused or repurposed, extending the life cycle of clothing and reducing the need for new resources.

Ethical fashion prioritizes fair labor practices and the welfare of garment workers. Brands that embrace this movement ensure that their production processes are transparent and that workers are paid fair wages and work in safe conditions. By supporting these brands, consumers can help drive positive change in the industry.

CHAPTER 5: SUSTAINABLE FASHION MOVEMENTS

These movements highlight the power of collective action. By making informed choices and advocating for sustainable and ethical practices, we can contribute to a fashion industry that is kinder to both the planet and its people.

6

Chapter 6: Innovations in Sustainable Materials

One of the most promising avenues for creating a more sustainable fashion industry lies in the development of eco-friendly materials. Innovations in this area are transforming how we think about fabric production and the resources it consumes.

Natural fibers like organic cotton, hemp, and bamboo are gaining popularity as sustainable alternatives to conventional materials. These crops require fewer pesticides and water, reducing their environmental footprint. Additionally, they are biodegradable, making them a more eco-friendly choice at the end of their life cycle.

Recycled materials are another exciting development. Fabrics made from post-consumer waste, such as plastic bottles and discarded clothing, offer a way to repurpose materials that would otherwise contribute to pollution. Innovations in this field are continually improving the quality and versatility of recycled textiles.

Biodegradable and bio-based materials are also making waves in the fashion industry. Fabrics made from algae, mushroom leather, and even lab-grown silk offer sustainable alternatives to traditional textiles. These materials often require fewer resources to produce and can break down naturally, reducing waste.

CHAPTER 6: INNOVATIONS IN SUSTAINABLE MATERIALS

Supporting brands that invest in sustainable materials is a powerful way for consumers to drive change. By choosing eco-friendly fabrics, we can reduce the environmental impact of our clothing and encourage the industry to adopt more sustainable practices.

7

Chapter 7: The Role of Technology in Fashion

Technology is playing a pivotal role in transforming the fashion industry towards more sustainable practices. From innovative design tools to advanced manufacturing processes, tech-driven solutions are helping to reduce the industry's ecological footprint.

3D printing is revolutionizing garment production by allowing designers to create intricate pieces with minimal waste. This technology enables precise material usage, reducing fabric scraps and offcuts. It also opens up new possibilities for customization and on-demand production, which can decrease overproduction and excess inventory.

Digital design tools are streamlining the creative process, enabling designers to visualize and modify their creations without the need for physical prototypes. This reduces the resources consumed in the development stage and allows for more efficient pattern-making and fabric usage.

Blockchain technology is enhancing transparency in the supply chain. By providing a secure and immutable record of each step in the production process, blockchain allows consumers to trace the origins of their clothing and verify ethical practices. This increased transparency fosters trust and accountability within the industry.

Artificial intelligence (AI) is also making its mark. AI-driven algorithms

CHAPTER 7: THE ROLE OF TECHNOLOGY IN FASHION

can predict fashion trends, optimize inventory management, and personalize shopping experiences. These innovations can help reduce waste, improve efficiency, and create a more sustainable fashion ecosystem.

8

Chapter 8: The Power of Consumer Choice

Consumers hold significant power in shaping the fashion industry. Our purchasing decisions influence production practices, labor conditions, and environmental impact. By making conscious choices, we can drive demand for more sustainable and ethical fashion.

One of the most effective ways to support sustainable fashion is by prioritizing quality over quantity. Investing in well-made, durable garments reduces the need for frequent replacements and lowers overall consumption. Timeless, versatile pieces that can be worn in various ways extend the life of our wardrobe and reduce waste.

Shopping secondhand is another impactful choice. Thrift stores, consignment shops, and online platforms offer a treasure trove of pre-loved clothing. By giving garments a second life, we reduce the demand for new production and minimize the environmental footprint of our wardrobe.

Supporting local and independent designers is another way to foster sustainable fashion. These creators often prioritize quality, craftsmanship, and ethical production methods. By choosing to invest in their work, we contribute to a more diverse and sustainable fashion ecosystem that values artistry and fairness.

Awareness is key to making informed decisions. Understanding the

CHAPTER 8: THE POWER OF CONSUMER CHOICE

origins of our clothing, the materials used, and the labor conditions involved empowers us to make choices that align with our values. Many brands now provide transparency reports and certifications, such as Fair Trade and Global Organic Textile Standard (GOTS), to help consumers navigate the complex landscape of sustainable fashion.

Ultimately, the choices we make as consumers send a powerful message to the industry. By prioritizing sustainability and ethics in our purchasing decisions, we can drive meaningful change and support a fashion industry that respects both people and the planet.

9

Chapter 9: The Role of Fashion Brands

Fashion brands play a crucial role in shaping the industry's impact on the environment and society. As key players in the supply chain, they have the power to set standards for sustainability and ethics. Many forward-thinking brands are already leading the charge towards a more responsible fashion industry.

One way brands can contribute to sustainability is by adopting circular economy principles. This involves designing products with their entire life cycle in mind, from sourcing sustainable materials to ensuring that garments can be recycled or repurposed at the end of their use. Brands like Patagonia and Eileen Fisher have pioneered circular fashion initiatives, demonstrating that sustainability and profitability can go hand in hand.

Transparency is another essential aspect. Brands that are open about their production processes, labor practices, and environmental impact build trust with consumers. By providing detailed information about their supply chain, companies can hold themselves accountable and encourage others to follow suit. Platforms like the Fashion Transparency Index rank brands based on their openness, helping consumers make informed choices.

Innovation is also driving change in the industry. Brands are investing in research and development to create sustainable materials, improve manufacturing processes, and reduce waste. For example, Stella McCartney has championed the use of eco-friendly materials and cutting-edge technology

CHAPTER 9: THE ROLE OF FASHION BRANDS

to create stylish, sustainable collections. By embracing innovation, brands can lead the way towards a more sustainable future for fashion.

10

Chapter 10: The Importance of Ethical Sourcing

Ethical sourcing is a critical component of sustainable fashion. It involves ensuring that the materials and labor used in production are sourced in a way that respects both people and the planet. This commitment to ethics can profoundly impact the entire supply chain, from farmers and textile workers to consumers.

One aspect of ethical sourcing is the use of fair trade practices. Fair trade certification ensures that producers receive fair wages, work in safe conditions, and have access to social benefits. This empowers communities and promotes economic development in regions where labor rights are often neglected. By supporting fair trade brands, consumers can help uplift marginalized workers and create a more equitable fashion industry.

Sourcing sustainable materials is another crucial element. Organic cotton, for example, is grown without synthetic pesticides and fertilizers, reducing environmental harm and protecting farmers' health. Similarly, materials like Tencel, made from sustainably harvested wood pulp, offer eco-friendly alternatives to conventional textiles.

Ethical sourcing also involves reducing waste and minimizing the environmental impact of production. This can be achieved through practices like zero-waste pattern making, which optimizes fabric usage to eliminate scraps.

CHAPTER 10: THE IMPORTANCE OF ETHICAL SOURCING

Brands can also implement recycling programs, encouraging consumers to return old garments for repurposing or recycling.

By prioritizing ethical sourcing, brands can create a positive ripple effect throughout the supply chain. Consumers, in turn, can support these efforts by choosing products that align with their values and advocating for greater transparency and accountability in the fashion industry.

11

Chapter 11: The Future of Fashion

The future of fashion lies in the hands of both industry leaders and consumers. As awareness of the environmental and ethical challenges grows, there is a collective push towards more sustainable and responsible practices. This shift is paving the way for a fashion industry that prioritizes the well-being of people and the planet.

One exciting development is the rise of regenerative agriculture. This approach goes beyond sustainable farming by actively restoring and enhancing ecosystems. Techniques like crop rotation, cover cropping, and reduced tillage improve soil health, increase biodiversity, and sequester carbon. By sourcing materials from regenerative farms, fashion brands can contribute to a healthier planet.

The integration of technology and sustainability is another promising trend. Innovations like biodegradable fabrics, smart textiles, and 3D knitting are transforming how we produce and consume clothing. These technologies offer new possibilities for reducing waste, conserving resources, and creating garments that are both stylish and sustainable.

Collaboration is key to driving meaningful change. Brands, consumers, governments, and NGOs must work together to establish industry-wide standards and regulations that promote sustainability and ethics. Initiatives like the Fashion Pact, a global coalition of brands committed to environmental goals, demonstrate the power of collective action.

CHAPTER 11: THE FUTURE OF FASHION

Ultimately, the future of fashion depends on our willingness to reimagine the industry. By embracing innovation, supporting sustainable practices, and advocating for systemic change, we can create a fashion industry that is kinder to both people and the planet. The journey towards a better world through fashion is not easy, but it is a path worth taking.

12

Chapter 12: Fashion Activism and Advocacy

Fashion activism and advocacy are powerful tools for driving change within the industry. Activists and advocates use their voices, platforms, and creativity to raise awareness about environmental and ethical issues, inspiring others to take action.

One influential movement is the Fashion Revolution, which emerged in response to the Rana Plaza tragedy. Fashion Revolution Week, held annually in April, encourages consumers to ask brands, "Who made my clothes?" This simple question promotes transparency and accountability, urging brands to disclose information about their supply chains and labor practices.

Social media has become a vital platform for fashion activism. Influencers, bloggers, and everyday consumers use their online presence to highlight sustainable and ethical brands, share information about industry practices, and advocate for change. Campaigns like #WhoMadeMyClothes and #BuyLessDemandMore have gained traction, amplifying the voices of those calling for a more responsible fashion industry.

Collaboration between activists, brands, and organizations is crucial for driving systemic change. Initiatives like the Sustainable Apparel Coalition and the Ethical Fashion Initiative bring together diverse stakeholders to develop and implement industry-wide standards and practices. By working

CHAPTER 12: FASHION ACTIVISM AND ADVOCACY

together, we can create a more just and sustainable fashion ecosystem.

13

Chapter 13: Redefining Luxury Fashion

Luxury fashion has long been associated with exclusivity, opulence, and high price tags. However, the concept of luxury is evolving to encompass sustainability and ethics. Modern consumers are increasingly valuing quality, craftsmanship, and the social and environmental impact of their purchases.

Leading luxury brands are embracing this shift by incorporating sustainable practices into their operations. For example, Gucci's Equilibrium initiative focuses on reducing the brand's environmental footprint, promoting diversity and inclusion, and supporting communities. Similarly, luxury conglomerate LVMH has committed to sustainability goals, including reducing greenhouse gas emissions and implementing eco-friendly practices across its brands.

Artisanal craftsmanship is becoming a hallmark of sustainable luxury. Brands that prioritize traditional techniques and handmade products often have lower environmental impacts and support skilled artisans. This approach not only results in high-quality, unique pieces but also preserves cultural heritage and promotes economic development in artisan communities.

Consumers play a pivotal role in redefining luxury fashion. By choosing brands that prioritize sustainability and ethics, they can drive demand for products that align with their values. This shift in consumer preferences is encouraging luxury brands to adopt more responsible practices, paving the

CHAPTER 13: REDEFINING LUXURY FASHION

way for a future where luxury and sustainability go hand in hand.

14

Chapter 14: The Impact of Fashion on Culture

Fashion is a powerful cultural force that shapes and reflects our identities, beliefs, and values. It serves as a medium for self-expression, creativity, and social commentary. Throughout history, fashion has played a pivotal role in cultural movements and societal change.

From the suffragette movement to the civil rights era, clothing has been used as a tool for protest and empowerment. Fashion allows individuals and groups to make statements about their beliefs, challenge norms, and advocate for change. Iconic styles and garments, such as the flapper dress or the black leather jacket, have become symbols of rebellion and social progress.

Fashion also has the power to unite and celebrate diverse cultures. Traditional attire, fabrics, and techniques from around the world contribute to the rich tapestry of global fashion. By embracing and honoring these cultural influences, the fashion industry can promote inclusivity, respect, and appreciation for diversity.

In today's interconnected world, fashion is more accessible and influential than ever. Social media, global travel, and cultural exchange have blurred the lines between local and global fashion trends. This interconnectedness offers opportunities for cross-cultural collaboration and innovation, fostering a more inclusive and dynamic fashion landscape.

15

Chapter 15: Education and Empowerment in Fashion

Education is a cornerstone of creating a more sustainable and ethical fashion industry. By equipping individuals with the knowledge and skills to make informed choices, we can drive positive change and empower future generations of consumers, designers, and industry leaders.

Fashion education should emphasize sustainability, ethics, and social responsibility. Many design schools and universities are incorporating these principles into their curricula, preparing students to address the industry's challenges. Courses on sustainable design, ethical sourcing, and circular economy principles equip students with the tools to create fashion that respects people and the planet.

Empowering garment workers and artisans is also essential for fostering a fair and just fashion industry. Providing access to education, training, and resources enables workers to improve their skills, advocate for their rights, and secure better opportunities. Organizations like the Ethical Fashion Initiative and Fair Trade advocate for the empowerment of workers, promoting economic development and social justice.

Consumer education is equally important. By raising awareness about the environmental and ethical impacts of fashion, we can encourage more responsible consumption habits. Workshops, seminars, and online resources can help consumers understand the complexities of the industry and make choices that align with their values.

Through education and empowerment, we can cultivate a generation of conscious consumers and industry leaders who prioritize sustainability and ethics. This collective knowledge and awareness will drive the fashion industry towards a more responsible and equitable future.

16

Chapter 16: Fashion's Role in Climate Action

The fashion industry has a significant impact on the environment and is a major contributor to climate change. However, it also has the potential to be a powerful force for climate action. By adopting sustainable practices and reducing its carbon footprint, the fashion industry can play a vital role in combating climate change.

One critical area is the reduction of greenhouse gas emissions. The fashion industry is responsible for approximately 10% of global carbon emissions. To address this, brands are adopting strategies such as using renewable energy, optimizing transportation and logistics, and improving energy efficiency in manufacturing processes. Additionally, initiatives like the Fashion Industry Charter for Climate Action aim to unite the industry in reducing emissions and setting science based targets.

Sustainable materials and practices are essential for reducing the industry's environmental impact. Brands are exploring alternative fibers, such as organic cotton, hemp, and recycled materials, which have lower carbon footprints compared to conventional textiles. Implementing circular economy principles, such as designing for longevity and recycling, can also help minimize waste and resource consumption.

Collaboration and innovation are key to driving climate action in fashion.

Partnerships between brands, governments, and NGOs can facilitate the development and adoption of sustainable practices. Investment in research and development can lead to breakthroughs in eco-friendly materials and technologies, further reducing the industry's environmental impact.

Consumers also have a role to play in supporting climate action. By choosing brands that prioritize sustainability and advocating for systemic change, we can drive demand for fashion that respects the planet. Together, we can create a fashion industry that contributes to a healthier and more sustainable future.

17

Chapter 17: Conclusion - Fashioning a Better World

The journey towards a more sustainable and ethical fashion industry is complex and multifaceted. It requires the collective efforts of brands, consumers, workers, and policymakers to drive meaningful change. By reimagining how we produce, consume, and dispose of clothing, we can create a fashion industry that respects both people and the planet.

As consumers, we hold significant power to influence the industry. By making conscious choices, supporting sustainable brands, and advocating for transparency and accountability, we can drive demand for ethical and eco-friendly fashion. Every purchase is an opportunity to support practices that align with our values and contribute to a better world.

Brands and industry leaders must continue to innovate and collaborate, adopting sustainable practices and prioritizing the well-being of workers and the environment. Transparency, ethical sourcing, and circular economy principles are essential for creating a fashion industry that is both profitable and responsible.

Education and empowerment are critical for fostering a generation of conscious consumers and industry leaders. By equipping individuals with the knowledge and skills to make informed choices, we can drive positive change and ensure a sustainable future for fashion.

Together, we can fashion a better world. By embracing sustainability and ethics in our clothing choices, we can create a fashion industry that celebrates creativity, respects people, and protects the planet. The journey may be challenging, but the rewards are immeasurable – a healthier, more just world for all.

Fashioning a Better World: The Ecology and Ethics of What We Wear

In a world where fashion is a powerful expression of identity and culture, the impact of what we wear extends far beyond aesthetics. This book delves into the environmental and ethical complexities of the fashion industry, offering a comprehensive exploration of how our clothing choices affect the planet and its people.

Discover the rise of fast fashion and its toll on natural resources, from the staggering amounts of water needed to produce a single T-shirt to the pollution caused by synthetic fibers. Uncover the human cost behind the glamorous facade, as garment workers endure harsh conditions and unfair wages to meet the relentless demand for cheap, trendy clothing.

But amidst these challenges, there is hope. The book highlights the growing movements and innovations that are reshaping the industry. From sustainable materials and eco-friendly technologies to ethical sourcing and fair labor practices, it showcases the efforts of brands, consumers, and activists who are committed to making fashion a force for good.

Explore the power of consumer choice and the role of fashion brands in driving change. Learn about the importance of transparency, circular economy principles, and regenerative agriculture in creating a more sustainable future. Through education and empowerment, we can cultivate a generation of conscious consumers and industry leaders who prioritize the well-being of people and the planet.

"Fashioning a Better World" is not just a call to action but a roadmap for a fashion industry that celebrates creativity, respects human rights, and protects the environment. Join the journey towards a more just and sustainable world, one garment at a time.